West Chicago Public Library District
118 West Washington
West Chicago, IL 60185-2803
Phone # (630) 231-1552
Fax # (630) 231-1709

LEAFY CRITTERS

For Dexter and Billie

Leafy Critters

Blue Dot Kids Press
www.BlueDotKidsPress.com

Original English-language edition published in 2020 by Blue Dot Kids Press,
PO Box 2344, San Francisco, CA 94126, Blue Dot Kids Press is a trademark of Blue Dot Publications LLC.

Original English-language edition © 2020 Blue Dot Publications LLC
© 2017 Yvonne Lacet
Originally published under the title *Bladerbeesten* by Uitgeverij J. H. Gottmer/H. J. W. Becht bv, Haarlem,
The Netherlands; a division of Gottmer Uitgeversgroep BV

This English-language edition is published under exclusive license with Gottmer Uitgeversgroep BV.
Original English-language edition designed by Susan Szecsi

BLUE
DOT

Cataloging in Publication Data is available from the United States Library of Congress.
ISBN: 978-1-7331212-2-4

FSC
www.fsc.org

MIX
Paper from
responsible sources
FSC™ C136333

Printed in China with soy inks.
First Printing

Yvonne Lacet

LEAFY
CRITTERS

BLUE DOT KIDS PRESS

Leafy Critters

Hello, reader!

I like to use common materials from nature like leaves, flowers, twigs, and berries to create images that inspire creativity. As you look through this book, use your imagination. Look at things in a different way. Berries become eyes, leaves become wings, twigs become paws.

See which animal catches your eye and create it yourself! Or create something completely new. Check out the back of the book to learn how to make your own leafy critters!

What leafy critters do you see on these pages?

Can you make one yourself?

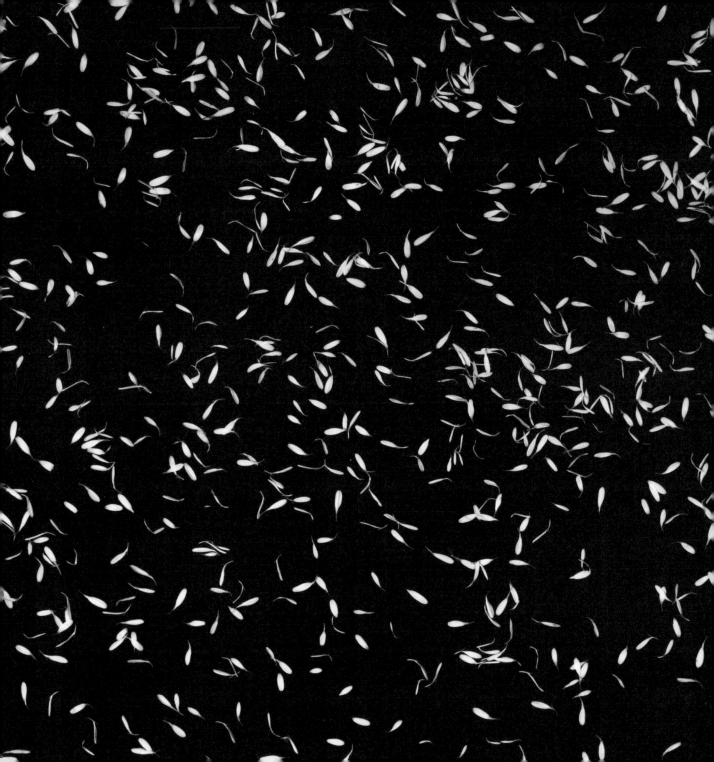

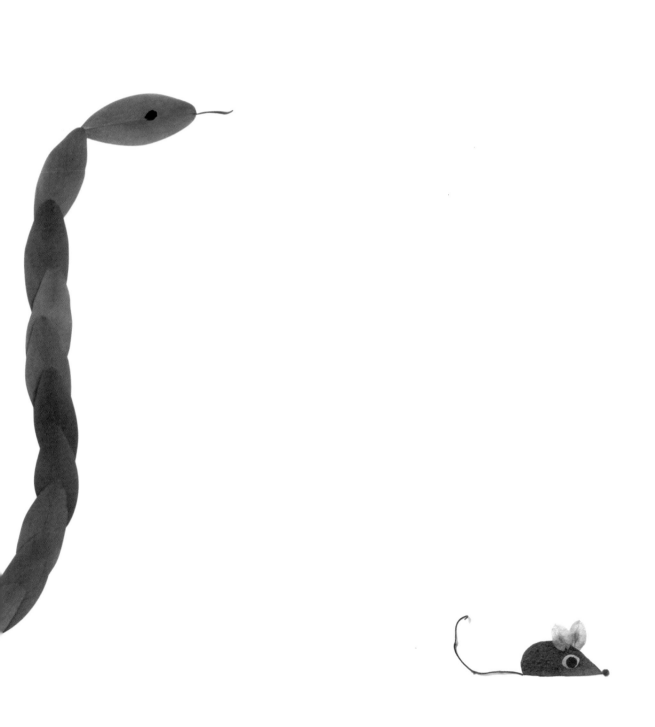

DIY

Gather

Leaves, twigs, flowers—anything you can find in nature
A blank piece of paper
A camera (optional)
Your imagination!

Collect

Look for the most beautiful, strange, unique materials. Search the park, the woods, or your garden. Collect materials that have different shapes, sizes, and colors. Remember to take only what you will use and follow park rules for foraging. Carefully place what you find between the pages of a book and take your collection home!

Imagine and create

Clear off a table to work on. Remove your treasures from the book and spread them out carefully. What do you see when you look at your collection? A mouse, perhaps? A fish, a butterfly, a tiger? Arrange some items on a piece of paper; move things around. A wonderful creature is surely hiding in there . . . Use your imagination and create the leafy critters you see!

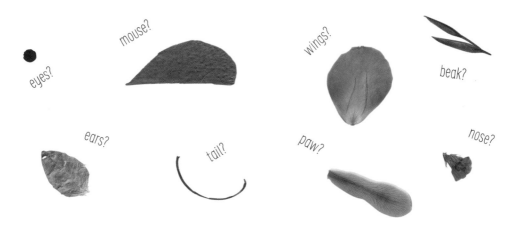

Share

Naturally, you will want to show everybody your leafy critter! There are some options to do that. Take a photo of your creation. You can even print it and put it up on the wall. Or frame your original art. Use a bit of glue and use thick paper to mount it.

About the Author

Yvonne Lacet is an internationally celebrated artist and a photographer who works on projects in which urban environments, the landscape, and nature play an important role. Her work has been internationally exhibited at locations such as the Chelsea Art Museum, in New York City, and the FOAM, in Amsterdam.